The
Divine Light
Invocation

The Divine Light Invocation

A Spiritual Practice for Healing and for
Realizing the Light Within.

Presented by
Swami Sivananda Radha

Box 50905, Palo Alto, CA 94303-0673
1990

TIMELESS BOOKS
Box 50905
Palo Alto, CA 94303-0673

Book design by Cynthia Poole
Photo credits: courtesy Yasodhara Ashram
                  Front cover photo of Swami Radha
                  courtesy Derek French

First edition published by Shiva Press 1966,1970,1976
Second edition published by Yasodhara Ashram Society 1987
This edition published by Timeless Books 1990
Printed in the United States of America

Library of Congress Cataloging-in-Publication Data:
Sivananda Radha, Swami 1911-
      The divine light invocation / presented by Swami Sivananda Radha.
         p.*89* cm. *21.5*
      ISBN 0-931454-17-4 : $10.95
      1. Spiritual life. 2. Light --Religious aspects. 3. Mantras.
      I. Title.
      BL624.S585   1990
      294.5'448--dc20   90-31896
                                                      CIP

The Divine Light Invocation Mantra

I AM CREATED BY
DIVINE LIGHT

I AM SUSTAINED BY
DIVINE LIGHT

I AM PROTECTED BY
DIVINE LIGHT

I AM SURROUNDED BY
DIVINE LIGHT

I AM EVER GROWING INTO
DIVINE LIGHT

In 1936 Swami Sivananda Saraswati founded the Divine Life Society for the purpose of sharing divine wisdom with all. Through his tremendous example the Yogic Teachings have become a living reality for thousands of people across the world.

To my Guru, Swami Sivananda Saraswati
and to all those who seek the Light.

Preface

In this time of great social and personal change in the world, acceptance of the spiritual aspect of our nature and of the spiritual teachings of all religions is becoming more and more urgent. People are slowly realizing that the only real hope for dealing with the problems facing the world is through transcending selfishness and narrow concerns of the ego in every one of us. It is the ego that creates the conflict and separation we experience. Peace and unity can only be attained by identification with the higher, spiritual dimensions of human nature. In discovering Inner Light we find the wholeness, the oneness and Light that we share with every other being in the cosmos. The one Light pervades all creation; all of the universe is one in the Light.

I have written this book to help you discover "the Light, that lighteth every man and woman that cometh into the World."(St. John) A short history is given of the events that occured when I was taught the Divine Light Invocation in India. Some explanations of the basic physical and psychological approaches that are used in Yoga, with preparatory exercises specifically connected to the Divine Light Invocation itself, are included. The actual Divine Light Invocation is described in a separate chapter. Because of the power of the Divine Light Invocation I strongly recommend the earlier chapters be read very carefully before practicing the Divine Light Invocation itself.

Through my extensive practice of the Divine Light Invocation in my own life, I have seen the results of this practice many times as a healing and purifying force for myself and others. I have also taught the Invocation to many who have found the power of the Light a real and effective force in their own lives and have been able to experience the healing and purifying effects of the Light for themselves.

Light has been a symbol for God, the divine energy, for many centuries in many religions. In the Bible, Jesus often makes reference to the Light: "I am the Way, the Truth, and the Light" and "If thine eye be single, thy whole body shall be full of light." Through constant and sincere practice of the Divine Light Invocation, you will come to a greater under-standing of your own divine nature and realize more fully the reality of the Christ-Consciousness within you.

As you practice the Divine Light Invocation, I pray that you may also become a channel for that cosmic energy, for the Light which is God, and share the Light with those in need wherever they may be.

Swami Sivananda Radha

Contents

Lead me from the unreal to the Real.
Lead me from darkness to Light.
Lead me from death to immortality.

Brihadaranyaka Upanishad

A Short History

During the fall of 1955 I flew to India to stay at the ashram of Swami Sivananda Saraswati, in the foothills of the Himalayas. Up until that time I had been living in Montreal, Canada. I had come to Montreal from Germany after the war and had been living and working there when I came into contact with my Guru, Swami Sivananda, through a visionary experience.

Since I could only obtain a six-month visa (three months plus an extension of three months) from the Indian government, my stay was extremely crowded. Swami Sivananda had scheduled virtually every minute of my day with spiritual practices. Toward the end of my stay, on February 2, 1956, I had the honor to receive an initiation from him into the ancient order of *sanyasa*—the path of renunciation and selfless service. The ceremony was performed by Swami Sivananda in a moment of inspiration and came to me as quite a surprise! One of the long-term residents at Sivananda Ashram remarked that he had never seen Master in such a high mood. He commented that "the sparks were literally flying!" After the initiation my previous name, Sylvia Hellman, was changed to Swami Sivananda Radha.

I was deeply moved by the whole sequence of events that had culminated in my sudden initiation. As the day passed the impact of these things deepened within me, and I felt the need to go and meditate upon the meaning of the new life I had just accepted. Near the Ashram, in the direction of the town of Rishikesh, were the ruins of an old temple, invisible from the road. How I found my way to this place I do not know, but while I was wandering among the tumbled down stones I felt an overpowering sense of familiarity. One tower of the original building had fallen over and there, half-buried in the sand, was a little cave-like shelter formed by an arch of the tower. I sat inside this cave and began to meditate when I became aware that there was someone standing near me.

The place where Babaji taught Swami Radha the Divine Light Invocation

I looked up. It was a man. At first there seemed to be nothing out of the ordinary about his appearance. I was about to take no notice of him when I realized that this was Babaji, the famous figure who had appeared to a number of spiritual aspirants in North India over the previous centuries. He radiated a great dignity, an aura and presence that were unmistakable to me.

At this point I would like to mention two incidents that occurred prior to the experience on the day of my initiation as a swami. About a year earlier I was in Montreal waiting for a group of yoga students in a downtown office building. While I was waiting, I was idly staring at a wall. Suddenly there appeared, as if projected, a scene of rocks and cliffs, half-shrouded in foliage. In the middle of the rocks I noticed a small cave, and from it emerged the figure of a man. He seemed to be in early middle age. I was struck by his tremendous dignity. He smiled, raised his hand, and made a beckoning gesture to me with his finger. The whole scene vanished as quickly as it had appeared, and I was left with a tremendous feeling of ecstasy, joy, and wonder . . . imbued with the presence of this person.

The second incident had taken place earlier during my stay in India. I was on the shore of the Ganges washing my clothes and thinking of the stories I had heard of Babaji. The stories had made such a strong impression on me that I had been meditating on Babaji, hoping that I might also be granted a meeting with him. I felt a special affinity for him. As I was washing I became aware of someone beside me. I looked up and saw an old man who had his head twisted to one side in a curious fashion, as though he did not want me to get a full view of his face. He took over the washing from me, with no objection on my part. Later when I thought about the incident, I realized it was quite peculiar to allow a stranger to take over a job like that from me. He asked what I was doing in India and what I had come in search of. I answered his questions but I had the distinct impression that he knew the answers before I spoke to him. I asked him who he was and he answered, "The one you are looking for." "Babaji?" I questioned. As I watched I saw him begin to drift out over the water and up into the air.

As he left me in this unusual manner, he said to me, "Any time you need help again to wash your dirty laundry, call on me." I was filled with that same sense of presence that I had experienced in Montreal, the same feeling of joy and awe.

I realized that the man who was before me at the temple ruins was the same person I had seen in Montreal and met beside the Ganges. It was now around sunset, and Babaji pointed into the distance. Suddenly he shouted, "Tiger!" Surprised and terrified, especially since tigers are no strangers to those parts, I froze, my breath bated and every muscle tensed. My senses were keyed to their utmost. He then told me to relax. There was no tiger. He explained he had used this means to show me that when one's concentration is at its height two things happen in the body—the muscles become tensed and the breath is suspended. He had produced this state in me by fear. He said that the same condition could be produced voluntarily and used for a specific purpose. He went on to show me and then to explain the Divine Light Invocation, and he taught me the Mantra for this practice. I performed the Invocation myself, and he showed me the technique for sharing the Light with another person. He asked me to name someone for this purpose. By this time I was so shaken by the experience that I could not think of a single person! He reassured me and told me to take just the outline of a human figure, which I did.

The first time I performed the Light Invocation I could

Twenty five years later, in 1982, Swami Radha revisits the place where Babaji once offered to assist her with her laundry.

very clearly see the Light flowing into me, while my eyes were closed. Babaji said that I should perform the Invocation in order to help others and also to break the habit of thinking of myself as either the mind or the body. The Light would help me to do so. He also told me that I should teach this to others. Then he bade me open my eyes, and in so doing I was dazzled by the sight of the Himalayas—the same Light that I had seen flowing through my own body was streaming out of the rock of the mountains.

When I saw this awe-inspiring vision my consciousness was suddenly swept up, as if by an enormous overpowering wave, to a level far beyond anything I had ever experienced. Words cannot describe what happened. My mind went beyond experience, and the body and personality of Swami Sivananda Radha were left behind, sitting in the toppled tower amidst the sand and rocks.

I owe my knowledge of what happened after this point to Mr. J. N. Khuller. He was a young Indian intellectual who had been sent by his family to stay at Sivananda Ashram in the hope that it would be good for his soul. He was a thorough modernist and because of his indifference, which bordered on contempt, for the traditional religious and moral practices, he had been a great trial to them. Not wanting to provoke a family crisis he had come to the Ashram, determined to put in his time as painlessly as possible and then return to the life he had mapped out for himself.

On this particular day he had gone to Rishikesh to visit some friends. They had just sat down to tea when he felt a powerful impulse to leave. He excused himself from the company, went outside, and began walking toward the Ashram. As he left Rishikesh he saw me staggering along the road, looking as if I were drunk. He came over and heard me chanting Om and talking about the Divine Light. It was obvious that I would need help in getting back to the Ashram, so he took me in hand as I was starting to cross one of the local bridges. At the request of Swami Chidananda, successor to Swami Sivananda as President of the Divine Life Society, Mr. Khuller later wrote a statement in which he described what happened that day:

We had passed the Andhra Ashram and were now nearing another bridge. This bridge had no protective railings. When we reached the bridge I was afraid she might fall off. I caught her hand and led her across. . . . Her hand! . . . Oh, it was hot, very hot! I had never seen anyone with such a high temperature still conscious. It was difficult to maintain a hold on her, such was the heat.

I knew she was on a different mental plane. I asked, "Do you recognise me Mother? Do you know who I am?" A smile spread on her lips. She said in a whisper, "Yes, I know you. But you do not know your own Self!" I was taken aback. In utter amazement I looked at her. Her face was now bright. It was actually luminous in the dark. Her eyes were fixed on the northern sky.

Suddenly she cried, "The Light! Don't you see it? High up. . . .the Light!"

"I cannot see it, Mataji," I said. She made no response and we continued walking. I was still supporting her.

Then she stopped. "LIGHT! See it, Jitendra . . . there!" I looked up to where she was pointing. There was nothing but the darkness of the night. Little stars were trying to pierce it with their feeble rays. There was nothing unusual or abnormal. Then the strangest thing in my life happened to me. I felt a sensation as if some current was flowing into my body through my arms. A strange current was flowing into my body from Mother Radha. I felt as if I was rising like a cloud out of my body . . . and then I saw IT! IT WAS THERE. LIGHT in the northern sky . . . bliss giving . . .soothing . . .bluish-white . . .penetrating . . .strong. Well, I cannot explain it. It is impossible to do so.

We made our way back to the Ashram. Mr. Khuller took me to my room and then went down to the main hall of the Ashram, where Swami Sivananda was attending *satsang*, the evening service, to tell him what had occurred. As far as we knew Swami Sivananda could have had no knowledge of what had happened to me since leaving the Ashram. Mr Khuller continued in his letter:

> *When I entered the hall, I saw his eyes fixed on the door as if waiting for me. He saw me and smiled. I felt as if he was silently asking me, "Alone?" I replied aloud, "Yes, Swamiji. Mother is in her room." All present laughed because to them I had said something in reply to no question at all. Gurudev [Swami Sivananda] asked me aloud, in a teasing way, "Why are you late today?"*
>
> *I was going to offer some explanation when he added, "Yes, but you have not wasted your time." It was then that I felt certain Gurudev knew everything. It was he who had blessed me by choosing me to witness and share in the divine experience of Mother Radha.*
>
> *Being a young Indian of the present generation I had stubbornly refused to accept anything like that. Now my belief was confirmed half an hour later at the close of satsang. We were going along with Swamiji to see him off to his kutir [living quarters]. Mother Radha met us on the way. The Master and Mother looked at each other for a minute without words, they had their own way of communication. Then the Master's eyes turned on me for a long time, after which he nodded his head and . . . smiled.*

I knew at that time that Swami Sivananda knew every thing that had happened that evening.

It was a long time before I even repeated the Divine Light Invocation. I had been given a number of spiritual practices to master by Swami Sivananda, and this took far longer than my very short stay in India. It was not until after my second journey to India, about three years later, that I began to practice the Divine Light Invocation on a regular basis. I did not want to teach the practice to others until I had thoroughly mastered it myself.

These events had a striking impact both on my life and that of Mr. J. N. Khuller. This experience and others like it have changed my life in directions I could never have imagined. The glimpse of Reality that I had been given through divine grace left me humble and more than ever determined to make myself worthy of what I had experienced, by striving to perfect my character and become one with my Higher Self. I have found that over a long period of time this gradual work on myself adds up to what amounts to a real transformation of being.

In the years that I have been practicing and teaching the Divine Light Invocation, I have seen many physical cures brought about through the power of the Light, as well as psychological and moral changes both in those who have practiced it and those with whom the Light has been shared. I pray that it will be as beneficial a form of spiritual practice for you in your life as it has been for me and that you will learn to share the Light with all those in need.

Jesus said to them:
Whoever has ears let him hear.
Within a man of light there is light and he
lights the whole world.

The Gospel According to Thomas, log 24

Identification: Who Are You?

When we ask ourselves who we are, why we exist, and what is important, the answers we often give are that money, possessions, power, status, or family are all we need to satisfy us. Yet we meet people in the world who have wealth, success, and status, and even these people, who have achieved what is meant to give them happiness and well-being in life, are often not satisfied. All of us ask ourselves at some time what the purpose of life is, why we were created. A vague sense of unease develops when we do not find satisfactory answers to these questions, and we avoid really confronting ourselves to find the truth. We look to books, to the mass media, to others' opinions for answers, in fact in every direction except the right one—inside ourselves.

The big problem for many people is not having a meaningful identification. Just who are you? With what do you want to identify? Your body? Then are you only a body if you identify with your body? If you are not the body, are you the mind? The mind has countless personality aspects. If you identify with the mind, you risk identifying with whichever aspect of your personality is foremost at that particular time. At any given moment this can shift to another personality aspect, and so you go, like a leaf in the wind, first in one direction and then in another, never knowing who you really are or where you are going. You will not find out who you are by selecting one personality aspect after another, experimenting to see which one fits best.

Once you accept the concept of a Higher Self, a soul, or Inner Light, then there is really nothing else with which you can identify. You become aware that all the other identities are transient; they change as you change. It is only the Light within you, the center that is God, that is eternal and unchanging.

What can we do? We have to begin by examining our habits of thinking. What do we mean by such terms as *God, cosmic energy, soul,* or *Higher Self?* Most of the time we use these words to refer to something outside ourselves. We are conditioned to accept separateness. We do not realize that we are always one with the Divine.

When I was first taught the Divine Light Invocation, I was unaware of my own habits of thinking. It was only after I had practiced and meditated upon the Light Invocation for some time that I came to understand its deeper meaning. For some years I used the Light Invocation only for myself; later on I used it for others. Some of the results startled me, especially when the person whom I had put into the Light did not know of it. Encouraged by these results, I began to introduce the Divine Light Invocation at lectures and meetings. Later I made a record and tape of the Light Invocation for people whom I could not teach personally.*

*See the *Divine Light Invocation*, cassette tape by Swami Radha.

Identification: Who Are You?

If divinity exists within us, then why do we need to invoke the Divine Light? Because we need to change our old habit patterns of identifying with the mind, the body, and the emotions. We need to realize in our heart, with our whole being, that we are all one in our divinity and only differ in our awareness of the oneness we share in the Light. We need help in changing our identification and instinctively we look outside to get this help. This habit has to be changed. We must learn that only from within ourselves can our true identification come.

We often look to others for that which only we can give ourselves—for example, love, strength, or purpose. When we realize our own divinity then we know all that we need is within ourselves. Identification outside ourselves is always false and misleading. Wrong identification is a major cause of marital problems, when one partner looks to the other to fill a need for love or direction, for example. Wholeness can only be discovered within oneself.

When the Divine Light Invocation is practiced with sincerity and diligence we come to accept the reality of the Light within us. By constant repetition of the Light Invocation we come finally to a direct, experiential realization that the world within and the world without are pervaded by the same Divine Light, the same cosmic energy. The more we pursue this practice, the deeper and clearer becomes this cosmic realization, the understanding of the cosmic essence that I AM.

To reach this point of new identification, of seeing and experiencing the Light that we share, that we are, we must change our symbolic images, eliminating those that cause a negative reaction within us. For example, we must stop reacting to another person's criticism. If we are critical of ourselves and have a poor self-image, this will manifest itself through criticism of others or a tendency to see everyone else as perfect. This must be changed if we are to grow and develop on the spiritual path. We need to cultivate imagination in the proper way, learn to relax and flow with the natural rhythms of our life, to become attuned to the divine will manifesting at each moment in our lives.

Identification with the Light within connects us to the divinity we share with others. When we put someone in the Light we give emphasis to that aspect of the other person that we share, going beyond the personality level of expression to the point where we are one in the Spirit and one in the Light.

By practicing the Divine Light Invocation, we can break the habit of looking outside ourselves for help, and we can stop our intentional blindness and open our eyes to our real nature, our true Self. By the exercise of will in practicing the Divine Light Invocation we create the right desire and, with the aid of our emotions, we can change this desire into a form that is subtle enough not to become an obstacle in our path to new realms of consciousness. The identification is raised above the level of imagery—in which cosmic energy is manifested in form, for example, as Jesus, the Buddha, or Lord Shiva—to the level of cosmic energy manifested as Light. At the point in our spiritual development at which it is no longer necessary to have an image of Light, we are able easily to transcend the image of Light because of its inherently subtle nature and to experience God beyond shape and form.

The image of Light gives the mind a form on which it may concentrate and focus for a sustained period of time. The Divine Light Invocation enables us to undo the habit of identifying with ourselves as either mind, body, or emotions. In essence we are none of these. We have minds and bodies, but what we are in truth is Spirit, God. A merely intellectual acceptance of this truth, although helpful at the beginning of our path, will not take us very far. The roots of old habits and identities have to be changed. Then we can have an intuitive comprehension of the answer to the question of who we are. We need to take time to reflect on our daily life, to take time to be holy.

Identification with the Light will help us to bypass the mental background noises—the inner dialogue of fantasy, fear, and doubt which is for most of us a constant companion. Doubt, in itself, is a healthy thing. Through doubt we can expand our awareness and understanding; but we need to be careful, since doubt can degenerate into confusion if it is carried on for too long. Doubt that is habitual, or derived from socially accepted beliefs, will prevent us from trying anything that is new and leave us without incentive to progress beyond our present state. We may end up unwilling to make any efforts to cooperate with our inevitable evolution, and then sooner or later we will be forced by circumstances to see what we need to learn.

The Divine Light Invocation is one of many spiritual exercises that exist for helping people to grow and increase their understanding of who they are. Different people have different temperaments, and no exercise will suit everyone. By all means try out many until you find the particular exercise that suits you. Then it is important to practice it regularly and in the right spirit until results are obtained. If we spend our lives looking here and there, without really settling for anything, we are doing little better than those who buy new things all the time to satisfy themselves. It becomes an endless search with no results. If we seem to spend our life just looking, tasting the spiritual smorgasbord available, it may be a signal that we are not really in earnest and are too weak to admit to ourselves our own lack of sincerity.

Most of the time we stand with our backs to our own Light, looking into the shadows. Once we become aware of our shortcomings, our defenses and problems, then what do we do about them? All too often our will seems to be powerless to eradicate traits that we ourselves recognize as undesirable. If you have done everything you thought was possible and still find yourself in the same dark spot, the Divine Light Invocation may give you the Light you need to see the way: "Seek ye first the Kingdom of God and all else shall be added unto you."* I would emphasize that it is your own experience and practice of the Divine Light Invocation that will give you an answer to the essential question, Who am I ?

* Matthew, 6:33

The light of the body is the eye:
if therefore thine eye be single,
thy whole body shall be full of light.

Matthew 6:22

Imagination

Wﾊ hat is imagination? Imagination is a powerful force of the mind, a faculty shaping every aspect of our lives, helping to determine the kind of people that we are, whether we are to be creative, neurotic, lazy, or energetic. Daydreaming is just one use of the faculty of imagination, often a rather negative and undisciplined one serving our frustrations and fantasies. By directing our daydreaming we can increase our creativity and begin to realize our true potential as human beings.

We must examine the sequence of imagination closely—the entire process, from the initial impulse, to the thought or idea associated with it, to the final image presented in our consciousness. What is the "it" that does the imagining? What is the "it" that does the thinking? The brain is only the material vehicle which serves to express "it."

Over the centuries, philosophers and scientists have gradually come to the startling conclusion that the whole objective universe is but a construction of consciousness, an edifice of conventional symbols shaped by the senses. Dr. Einstein carried this logic to its limits by showing that even space and time are forms of intuition, itself an aspect of consciousness. If the universe can be regarded as a continuously evolving creative thought, then could not the "it" we are trying to discover be a miniature replica of the mind that thinks this vast thought? "One mind, though many thinkers." Like an endless shower of sparks, dividing and ever-changing, the universe creates an infinite variety of new forms. So also within our own minds, myriad ideas, images, and inspirations manifest themselves. These exist not only in the conscious mind but also on other levels of awareness, many of which we may never be aware of.

Imagination can alter our lives at every level of our being once we realize the power it has. We can realize the peace within and reduce our anxiety by the correct use of imagination. Imagination serves desire, which leads on to new desire. Desire can be likened to clay in the potter's hands. When it is still pliable it can be molded into any shape or form, but once the final shape is made and it is fired in the kiln, it becomes unalterable. In the same way, once our desire is set and fired in the kiln of our emotional impulses, we are stuck with that form. It will help us, then, to look carefully at our ideas, our thought-forms, to see if they are what we really want. If not, we should hasten to change them and make new ones. We must not wait too long since we may find to our dismay that these habitual thought-forms have become as hard as rock. To change them at that point may prove to be a most difficult task.

Most of our deep-seated ideas are just such "hard rocks." Many are thought-forms that were imposed on us during our childhood, and that may have been useful in the past but are now obsolete. We need to consider if they are really useful in our lives today. In deciding which to retain or dispose of, we must use all our powers of discrimination. Those that have served a purpose in the past may well be an obstacle to our new growth. It is essential that discrimination be coupled with awareness if we are to progress in our spiritual development.

As we grow up, we become accustomed to thinking in terms of symbols and we react to symbolic images. We tend to have set reactions to national flags, uniforms, and outer appearances such as hair styles or clothing. It is important to see beyond symbolic images to essences rather than to mistake the symbol for the real. In Mantra Yoga, for example, the Mantra acts as a vehicle or vessel to carry the mind, and at a certain point the vehicle is no longer necessary. In the same way, we would not carry a boat on our shoulders after we had reached the other side of a lake; it would have served its purpose. This process of mistaken symbolism is quite apparent in the literal interpretations often given to Bible stories. When we use the symbol of Light we are using an inherently subtle image, one that can be easily transcended when it is no longer needed.

Words are frequently inadequate to follow our imagination as it weaves the tapestry of our vision of life. We customarily give certain meanings to words, attaching to them old, habitual images, thereby hindering communication with others. Most of the time words will show us only the reverse side of the tapestry of truth; the real design lies on the other side.

Negative or depressive moods can be seen as the result of an accumulation of negative, destructive symbolic images. Everyone can prove within the laboratory of her or his own mind the enormous waste of vital energy involved in the thinking and rethinking of such images, trying to control or limit their emotional consequences of fear, anger, anxiety, and so on.

We may take great care and have discrimination in what we feed our physical body, but how often do we discriminate about what we feed our mind? We let the inner dialogue run on and on, like a tape recorder playing the same tape over and over. The energy that we use for this can be used much more effectively, with no internal struggle, in the pursuit of a positive goal if we so choose. Using our power of choice, we can decide the kind of person we want to be: Edgar Cayce, the famous psychic, said, "As a man thinketh, so is he. . . They themselves are makers of themselves." He often spoke of "Mind the Builder" in reference to the power of the mind to create. Unless we exercise self-control, our imagination may run wild, as, for example, when hatred and resentment become projected onto someone of a different skin color.

"If thine eye be single, thy whole body shall be full of light." With one-pointedness of mind we are able to imagine what it would be like to become filled with Light. Light is a most positive and beneficial image to implant in the mind. Remember that it is practice that ultimately counts. We can exercise our power of choice by exposing our consciousness to higher influences, opening ourselves only to that which is divine, the Most High. By identifying with the Light we are able to do this. We must recognize that we can choose the kind of suggestion that we are going to accept into our consciousness, and we should do everything in our power to ensure that this influence is positive. By an act of will we can take hold of the freedom that is our birthright as human beings; we can make use of our power of choice. It is entirely up to each one of us.

The sun does not shine there,
nor the moon and the stars,
nor these lightenings, and much less this fire.
When That shines, everything shines after that.
By its Light all this is lighted.

Katha Upanishad 5:15

Exercises to Cultivate Imagination

I f you watch your mind you will become aware that every little stimulus sets off the power of imagination, resulting in numerous images. These appear so quickly that it becomes virtually impossible to be aware of them unless you make a special effort to do so. By their very detail and power these images can tell you not only about the power of your own imagination, but also where your awareness happens to be. Below is a series of exercises for the positive cultivation of imagination. Take each exercise in turn and practice it for yourself.

1. See yourself going through a complete day, beginning with the moment you awoke. For this you should place yourself in a very comfortable position. See yourself opening your eyes. Stretching will help you recapture that very first thought before you got up and began the activities that made up the day. Recall these activities and then ask yourself if there are any that you would change. Make a note of these. Later on, think of improvements.

2. Imagine a garden. Walk through it. Find your favorite flower. Keep your thoughts fixed on that flower as long as you can. Try one complete minute. Make it three

---

minutes, then five. To think of a flower for five solid minutes, even for one minute—that's real work, isn't it!

3. In your mind's eye you light a candle. Look at it for one, two, up to five minutes, excluding all other thoughts from your mind.

4. Look into a mirror, preferably one in which you can see yourself full-length. Focus your eyes on a point on your body such that you can see all of yourself. Now move closer to the mirror: your eyes shift with each move. Look at your face, at your eyes. Is that you? How do you look? Worried? Miserable? Hateful? Kind? Sweet? Gentle? Think about how you would like to look, making a list of those qualities and arranging them in order of importance. Can you then assemble all of these characteristics into a single image of yourself? Now, superimpose on your image in the mirror the image of Light. Is there a change in the expression of your eyes? Let the Light shine through your eyes. Let this Light be your giving of joy, trust, gentleness, and wisdom. You can use the following suggestion to reinforce this: The Light of God shines through my eyes.

5. Fix the image of the sun in your mind. (Never look directly at the sun.) Now feel its warmth. Can you feel this warmth inside as well as outside? Be conscious of all these impressions so that you can recall them when you need to.

6. Observe the relationship between the sun and your shadow. As the sun rises your shadow darkens and

shortens. At noon your shadow almost disappears. You can try this exercise indoors under a light bulb. Suspend a 150 or 200 watt bulb in the center of a room. Turn the light on and stand directly underneath it. You do not see the bulb itself, you see the light emanating from it. Now feel the gentle warmth that the light also gives off. Try to feel it all over your body. When you can do this easily, either with the sun or the light bulb, dispense with them and use your imagination alone.

7. After you are able to feel the light and warmth all over, in your mind's eye see the Light entering your body through the top of your head in the region of the fontanella. See the Light penetrating your entire body, right into your fingertips, right down to your toes. You are now seeing yourself in a shower of Light. Feel the warmth from the Light inside and outside.

8. Take the last line of the Divine Light Invocation Mantra and repeat it silently to yourself. Do so clearly, slowly, with every word distinct: I am ever growing into Divine Light.

Decide right then, "I shall persist in this practice until I have become a new person, seeing myself as one with the Light." Once this identification has taken place, you are on the way. A new you will have been created on every level of your being. But this creation must take place first in your own mind.

9. So far we have worked on the physical body; now we will bring Light into other levels of consciousness. To do so

you will again need the assistance of your imagination. Let the Light enter through the top of your head and flow into your spine. The vital force that keeps you alive is concentrated most strongly in your spine, where it constantly flows like electricity through wires. The peripheral nerves distribute these life impulses through out the body. In the yogic tradition the ancient wise men taught that the various levels of consciousness are located in a number of *chakras* or centers along the spine.

10. Imagine your spiritual heart as a big Valentine's heart with two doors in the center of your chest. At first they are closed. In your mind, open the doors as far as they can go: see your heart center wide open. It fills your whole chest, particularly after the doors have been opened. It gives you a feeling of generosity, doesn't it? You are giving of yourself. You are giving of the best you have. You give from the heart.

    Your actual physical heart should be ignored. Under no circumstances should you listen to your heartbeat or even think of your physical heart while doing this exercise. If you do so, you may interfere with its normal functioning. Realize that you are giving of yourself, which is much more than any tangible gift. The object is to mobilize emotions that will be helpful to your practice. Emotions need to be cultivated just as any other of your faculties. All of these exercises are aimed at developing your imagination and feelings in a positive direction.

11. With your eyes closed and focused on the space between the eyebrows, try to produce a spiral in your mind's eye.

Exercises to Cultivate Imagination

Then imagine a garden hose coiled up before you. Imagine there is light flowing upward through the hose. Dispense with the image of the hose and see a spiral of Light rising in front of you. Experiment with controlling this spiral of Light. See it spiral upward, higher and higher. See the spiral disappear into the sky. Continue this exercise until you can do it easily and smoothly.

12. See a friend standing in front of you. With the doors of your heart center open, a stream of Light flows outward. It goes to the feet of the person before you and forms a spiral encircling him or her. Imagine the spiral rising upward and carrying your friend with it. Visualize two people together. Let the Light encircle them both and lift them up together. Begin again, this time with a family group gathered closely together. Direct the spiral of Light to their feet and and see it wind clockwise around the whole group. See them all united in the Light. It is not at all necessary to visualize their faces one by one; simply see the outlines of human beings.

Such outlines of people can also be used when you want to help a stranger. For example, when you hear the siren of an ambulance you know that help is urgently needed. You can give help by means of the Divine Light Invocation. If you can give more support to your imagination by knowing that a man, woman, or child is in need, by all means use that image, but don't depend on it.

As time goes by you will find that the imagination, properly guided and directed, can become a wonderful tool for blessing yourself and others. If you feel depressed, burdened by doubt, worry, or uncertainty, place a beauitful, positive image in your mind. When your life is filled with Light there is hope. Hope gives strength, and strength is needed to carry on.

"All the world's a stage, and all the men and women merely players," wrote Shakespeare. We can choose the roles we are to play in life, and share in writing the script. Consider what image you have created of yourself and projected to others. Only you have the power to change the roles you find yourself playing in life. If you indulge in self-pity or avoid responsibility but do not like being that way, then make up your mind to change. Before making any changes in yourself you must first meditate on the question, What kind of a person do I want to be? Then proceed to change your self-image and keep yourself in the Light. Don't expect miracles. You have gone for years before sincerely desiring to change, but if you have patience and perseverance it will pay off. Take time to reflect on your daily life. Keep a spiritual diary and see how you are living up to your ideals each day.

Often we expect too much of others and not enough of ourselves. Some of us want to be appreciated for what we are, yet we cannot do the same for others. This is worth thinking about. The next time you make this demand of others, look at what you have to offer them. Renew yourself daily in the Light and be your own witness. Know that you are really one with the Light.

*For the commandment is a lamp
and the law is light;
and reproofs of instruction
are the way of life.*

Proverbs 6:23

Relaxation

Relaxation means being relaxed enough to see things in their true proportions, to see the facts with clear vision. Uncontrolled imagination can lead to exaggerations and distortions, giving energy to fantasies, which can in turn lead to a great deal of tension within the body. With the help of the exercises given below you can become aware of your tension and, with this awareness, begin to change yourself to become the kind of person you want to be.

Do you know when and where there is tension in your body? Check yourself for a moment. Is your neck tensed or relaxed? Spread your fingers and create the maximum degree of tension in your hands. Very slowly release that tension. Can you become aware of the moment of maximum tension? Try this same exercise with the other parts of your body. Become aware of even the slightest muscular and nervous reactions within your body, so that the tension can be released at the moment of awareness, in the here and now.

Emotional disturbances often manifest in the physical body as points of tension. Tension needs to be recognized and released; otherwise we lose our freedom and no longer act from our center, but instead react compulsively to the changes that life brings. Because of the close interdependence of mind and body, we can control our emotions by learning to control our body. In the same way, controlling our imagination will help us to control the tension we experience in our body. To be able to relax, it often helps to explore just where the tension is, to become aware of exactly where tension is located.

Experiences from the past that have accumulated tension may become locked in the body and in the mind, as symbolic images. As we begin to look at ourselves and identify with the Light, these images will dissolve and help us to release tension. We will feel more vital, energized. The energy that was previously wasted in fighting ourselves is released, and we can now decide how we want to use it creatively. Relaxation is both a cause and consequence of releasing attachment to our negative aspects. To find inner peace we must let go of the inner struggles, of identifying with old images, fears, and resentments. Put energy into the positive aspects of life. Identify with the Light that you are.

Will the tension be permanently released? This depends entirely on whether an awareness of our thoughts and actions is maintained. If the old habits are allowed to reassert themselves, then better knowledge and intentions will be defeated. Bad habits are not eradicated by acts of will alone, but by changing the images that support and represent them. We can mobilize our emotions and feelings to help develop a new identification for ourselves.

Did you know that when we are really afraid, every muscle of the body becomes tensed? We hold our breath and become "all ears." This simply means that the entire consciousness has been focused on the sense of hearing and all the other senses have faded into the background. In the Divine Light Invocation we attempt to reach a similar state of deep concentration by means of our will. In the Light Invocation we deliberately tense the body to increase concentration. Maximum tension implies its opposite, maximum relaxation. In the Divine Light Invocation we relax so that we can surrender to the Light and so to the divine will. Surrender is the very essence of relaxation. Tensing in the Light Invocation helps us to exclude thoughts that try to force their way into our consciousness, and to concentrate on the Mantra of the Light.

In a state of relaxation and non-resistance, intuitive thoughts can flow that may escape our awareness at other times. Relaxation means non-resistance, surrender. Life is a flow, and we can live life to the fullest only when we are flexible. This does not mean being spineless. We must know our limits and discriminate as to when it is important to take a stand. In the words of Lao Tsu,

> Yield and overcome,
> Bend and be straight,
> Empty and be full.

And Krishna says to Radha:
"Being a mass of Light, you are formless,
taking on a body to favor your devotees."

Brahmavaivarta Purana, Book II:55:78

Exercises for
Relaxation

While there are many exercises to relax the body and, in conjunction with the body, the mind, all exercises have a specific result in mind. It is important to learn not only to relax but also to create tension at will, in order to understand both functions. These exercises will help you get in touch with your areas of tension, and aid you in learning to relax. They are also intended as preparatory exercises for the practice of the Divine Light Invocation.

Stage One

1. Stand erect. Tense the feet as hard as you can. Feel every degree of the tension. Repeat this several times, until you develop an awareness of how each degree of tension and relaxation feels.

2. Let the arms hang loose. Slowly tense the hands, spreading the fingers apart. Notice how the tension spreads up the arms. Slowly relax the hands. Repeat this several times until you again develop an awareness of the first moment of tension, and of all the degrees of tension and relaxation.

3. Coordinate the tension and relaxation of the hands and feet. Tense them together and relax them together. Repeat

this until it becomes easy. Try to prevent any reflection of this tension to other parts of the body; keep all parts of the body relaxed except where tension is specifically requested.

4. Beginning with tensing the hands, extend the tension to the forearms. Let relaxation follow after each tensing, in the same order in which you tensed; that is, relax the hands first, forearms next. Repeat the previous step with the feet and calves. Coordinate the tensing of the hands and forearms with the tensing of the feet and calves. Tense . . . relax. Tense . . . relax.

5. Starting with tensing the hands, extend the tension first into the forearms, then into the upper arms. Slowly relax. Repeat the previous step with the feet, calves, and thighs. Coordinate the tensing of the hands, forearms, and upper arms with the tensing of the feet, calves, and thighs. Gently relax.

6. Tense the hands, forearms, upper arms, and now the shoulders as well. Gently relax. Tense the feet, calves, thighs, and buttocks. Relax—always in the same order in which you tensed, that is, feet, calves, thighs, and lastly buttocks. Coordinate tensing hands, forearms, upper arms, and shoulders with feet, calves, thighs, and buttocks. Tense and relax.

7. Tense just the abdomen. Relax. Tense the neck. Relax. Coordinate the successive tensing of the feet, calves, thighs, buttocks, and abdomen with that of the hands, forearms, upper arms, shoulders, and neck. Slowly tense and slowly relax in the same order. Repeat this coordinated

tensing and relaxing until it becomes easy:
1. Hands—feet
2. Forearms—calves
3. Upper arms—thighs
4. Shoulders—buttocks
5. Neck—abdomen

Make sure that your face and head remain relaxed at all times during these exercises.

Stage Two

Now we can incorporate controlled breathing into the exercise:

As you tense, inhale.
Hold the tension and retain the breath.
As you relax, exhale.

This can be mastered in several stages. As you inhale, tense the whole body beginning with the hands and feet. Hold the breath and the tension, then exhale and relax at the same time. Go through all of the exercises until you have mastered the coordination of tensing-inhaling, holding the tension-holding the breath, and exhaling-relaxing. Increase the length of time you hold the breath in gradual stages. There should never be any strain or pressure felt in the body.

Stage Three

Inhale and tense the whole body smoothly. Do not strain. Retain the breath and tension only for as long as it feels comfortable. Relax and exhale slowly, experiencing clearly each degree of tension and relaxation.

We are not cut off or severed from the Light,
but we breathe and consist in it'
since it is what it is.
In the moment of union, we are able
to see both Him and ourselves -
ourselves in dazzling splendor, full of
spiritual Light,
or rather one with the pure Light itself.

Plotinus

The Divine Light
Invocation

A fter thoroughly practicing the relaxation exercises given in the previous chapter, you are ready for the actual Divine Light Invocation.

Stand erect, feet shoulder-width apart. Lift the arms above the head at the same time as you smoothly and gradually tense the whole body. The arms should be kept straight and the tension maintained throughout the body. Hold the tension and the breath. Keep the eyes closed and focus them on the space between the eyebrows. Make the following affirmation to yourself, silently and with all the concentration possible:

> I am created by Divine Light
> I am sustained by Divine Light
> I am protected by Divine Light
> I am surrounded by Divine Light
> I am ever growing into Divine Light*

Use your imagination to *see* yourself standing in a shower of brilliant white Light. See the Light pouring down upon you,

---

*The final line of the Divine Light Invocation is not part of the original Mantra given by Babaji. I have added it as an affirmation for the direction of the will.

The Divine Light Invocation

flowing into the body through the top of the head, filling your
entire being. Then slowly lower the arms. Now, without raising
the arms, keeping them at your side, tense the body and inhale.
Hold the tension and the breath. Mentally repeat the Invocation. Slowly exhale and relax.

These two stages are shown in figures 1 and 2 on page
41.

During the second repetition, with the arms beside the
body, concentrate on *feeling* a warm glow of Light suffuse your
entire body, outside as well as inside. Acknowledge silently to
yourself:

*Every cell of this, my physical body, is filled with Divine
Light. Every level of consciousness is illumined with Divine Light.
The Divine Light penetrates every single cell of my being, every
level of consciousness. I have become a channel of pure Light. I am
one with the Light.*

The Divine Light Invocation is an exercise of will as well
as an act of surrender. Be receptive to the Light and accept that
you are now a channel of Divine Light. Express your gratitude
with deep feeling. Have the desire to share this gift with
someone whom you wish to help. Turn your palms forward as
shown in figure 3 on page 41.

You can now share the Divine Light with any friend or
relative. See him or her standing before you. Mentally open the
doors of your heart center and let the Light stream forth
toward the feet of this person. The Light encircles the person
and spirals upward in a clockwise direction, enveloping the

body completely. See the spiral moving high up into the sky, taking his or her image along with it. Finally the person merges into the source of the Light and becomes one with the Light. You may even lift your head to follow the spiral of Light, keeping the eyes closed. When the person has passed from your view, relax and silently give thanks for having the opportunity to help someone in need. Remember, in helping others we are helping ourselves.

You are now ready to begin all over again, putting others into the Light, one by one, in the same way. As you become more familiar with the Invocation, take several people in a group or a family together. If you should want to help many people, you must renew the complete Light Invocation as soon as you notice that your attention begins to slacken.

If you wish to help someone not known to you directly, just imagine the outline of a person of the appropriate sex. Or you can put strangers into the Light—people unknown to you but who are in need of the Light—by just imagining a figure. Your efforts will not be in vain.

You can also see projects or abstract ideas in the Light. Be sure that the ideas are always positive: see peace, love, or harmony in the Light, never war, disease, or poverty.

Do not let your right hand know what your left hand is doing. Give with humility. Put a seal upon your lips and forget what you have done.

If the person whom you are trying to help prefers to know that you are concerned for him or her, arrange a set time

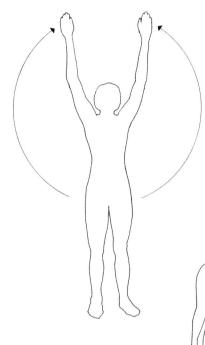

1. *"Stand erect, feet shoulder-width apart. Lift the arms above the head..."*

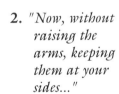

2. *"Now, without raising the arms, keeping them at your sides..."*

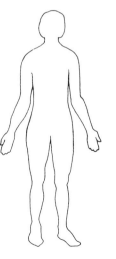

3. *"Mentally open the doors of your heart center..."*

for performing the Light Invocation and ask the individual to be in a state of relaxation and receptivity at that time.

The Divine Light Invocation may also be used as a Mantra. Repeat the words of the Invocation to yourself and see yourself surrounded by Divine Light in your daily life. It will help you to keep in touch with the Light within you and to see the Light in others around you.

Before you go to sleep each night, see your body and bed surrounded by a spiral (like a cocoon) of Divine Light. In this way your physical body, which is the temple of your soul, will be protected so that the soul can do its work in safety.

The Divine Light Invocation may be used to bless any friends or relatives who have died. When you put them into the Light see them as they were when they were at their very best in the physical body before their transition. See them surrounded and filled with Light. This will help you to release any attachment to them, and will also help them on their path on the other side.

It is very important, before you put another person in the Light, that you first put yourself thoroughly in the Light. The Light Invocation has to be meaningful; never allow it to become routine. When water runs through a rusty pipe, the water comes through, but with it comes much else that is unwanted. In the same way that the water running through a rusty pipe will finally clean it out, so through your efforts you become more spiritual, a purer channel for the Light. As you keep practicing, the channel will become clearer. This is a form of selfless service.

Many people have written and told me of their experiences with the Light Invocation. I have given three of these below.

"In New York I had one week to rehearse with my pianist and put together the chamber works on the program. I really worked on seeing everyone in the Light and seeing myself as a channel for the Light. When the recital finally came I felt beautifully calm, collected, and prepared. I gave my ego to God beforehand and worked on seeing the audience in the Light and seeing myself as a channel for sharing the Light. I felt the Light flowing through me and felt the presence of friends sending me Light. I was sustained, protected, and surrounded by divine energy and Light for that recital. One of my friends said that when she closed her eyes she saw me in the Light, surrounded by bright Light. I have enclosed a review of the recital. Needless to say, it is spectacular. I am grateful to God."

"I have tried to remember to always identify with the Light, and it has worked very well for getting me out of those deep depressions. I have been doing the Light Invocation at least once a day or when I needed to. . . . I have more energy, feel better, and am much more optimistic about everything! I seem to be able to see the Light and certainly can feel a very strong something—there is some current pulling forward so I can hardly stand up at times. Then I feel myself slipping away as if floating up and leaving nothing behind. There is a sound like a waterfall coming up louder and louder into my head. Then it becomes a buzzing and ends up a humming. It seems to be inside pressing out as well as pressing in from outside. Then I feel I am no longer there, but that I must lie down before I fall down. At the same time I see, with my eyes open or closed, a bright blinding thing in front of

me: it is sort of oval-shaped and has a whirling centre of Light energy, and it doesn"t fade completely for about twenty minutes."

In a research paper on Life Energies, presented by Dr. Harold Streitfield at the First International Congress of Parapsychology and Psychotronics in Prague, he describes his experience with the Divine Light Invocation.

"Once I felt (the Light) so strong it seemed as though I had a miner's headlamp on. I find such a meditation on the Light the most valuable kind I can do now .... I especially like the one given to us by Swami Radha. This is an ancient Mantra which goes as follows:

I am created by Divine Light. I am sustained by Divine Light. I am protected by Divine Light. I am surrounded by Divine Light. I am ever growing into Divine Light."

The preceding chapters are intended as a commentary to aid you in understanding this one, especially if spiritual practice is new to you. They can only give you clues or hints. In the final analysis you must draw your own conclusions from your experience and practice. If you practice the Divine Light Invocation regularly you will receive fresh insights as to how it may be used. Listen to these insights and apply them. Only if you persist will you achieve results that will convince you far more effectively than anything I could write.

Then shall thy light break forth
as the morning,
and thine health
shall spring forth speedily.

Isaiah 58:8

The
Divine Light Invocation
for Healing

The Divine Light Invocation aims at activating the healing forces latent within every one of us. It brings Light to all levels of consciousness, emphasizing the positive side of our nature and taking energy away from the negative—the resentments, complaints, and self-pity we hang onto and identify with. Sort out the positive and the negative within yourself. Give emphasis to the positive, go beyond your past mistakes and future fantasies, fill the mind with positive images.

It has often been said that the faults we despise in others are the faults we cannot accept in ourselves. That is exactly why we criticize them in others. Once you deal with them in yourself, you will discover a greater peace and love in your relationships with others. As inside, so outside. You are the only person responsible for all the things you complain about. If you are honest with yourself, you could probably write a list of those things that others might complain about in you. If you can't, then begin observing yourself.

When the Light Invocation is done with goodwill it removes feelings of hostility between couples or others who have problems. If you have a problem with criticism, apologize and put the other person in the Light. We don't always want to admit that we are wrong, but if we are to grow spiritually then habitual criticism has to go.

What is it that heals? All of us have a certain amount of healing power within our own bodies. Light is a symbol for the force that heals. By seeing yourself and others in the Light you will mobilize those invisible forces that are the gift and property of every human being. The Light can heal us.

To help bring about the healing of another person you must become thoroughly familiar with the practice of the Divine Light Invocation set out in the previous chapters. The person or people whom you wish to heal should always be seen in the mind's eye standing in front of you healthy and whole. Even if the person is in bed or a wheelchair, always see his or her image standing upright in the Light, healthy and whole.

Some healing is instantaneous, but more often the Divine Light Invocation must be done repeatedly over an extended period of time before results are seen. Medical advice and treatment should be sought if necessary, and the doctor should be seen as a channel for the Light. We must always see ourselves cooperating with the laws of nature. Help yourself and others to unfold according to the divine plan. See the Light as helping the sick person to open himself or herself to a greater understanding and acceptance of God's will and healing grace. Sometimes a spontaneous healing can come simply to show an individual that there is some truth in these things. But it is very serious if the person does not follow this up by changing his or her life.

If you are going to help others you must learn to be aware, to preserve your energy, and to be a pure channel for the Light. Becoming more sensitive to others and their needs helps you to heighten perception and understanding and is the first step in becoming more sensitive spiritually.

However, becoming more sensitive can also make you more vulnerable to being drained of energy by others. In situations such as social gatherings, where it is easy to be drained of energy, you can protect yourself by surrounding yourself with Light. By doing so you will also become a silent source of blessing to those you meet.

People often identify with the one they are helping. You should only identify with the Light. To put this in a nutshell, if you had to have your appendix taken out and I were your surgeon, and if I were to identify with the pain that my knife would give you, I might waver and injure you instead of doing a good job. But when you identify with the Light, you become a channel of Light; then anything is possible.

The practice of the Divine Light Invocation even before approaching a person in physical or emotional need will put the helper into the right frame of mind: cheerful, hopeful—in other words, positive.

The great spiritual teachers all agree that the highest form of giving is silent and anonymous. There is one exception to this as it applies to the Divine Light Invocation. At certain times it may help the one being healed to know that the Light is being sent. If this is the case let the individual know; otherwise always work silently.

See yourself as a channel for the Light, through which the healing force can flow. Do not consider yourself a healer. It is the Light that heals. Imagine yourself as a channel, giving support and direction to the Light, just as a wire channels the electricity flowing through it.

Through the Divine Light Invocation you can help without telling the Divine what to do. You can't say, "I want my friend to get better. I want my mother to be healed. I want my child to be well." It is not up to you. You do not know what is best for any individual.

Know that the more you give, the more you receive. Be grateful. Gratitude is one of our finest feelings. If properly cultivated, gratitude will bring many blessings. As channels for the Light we are blessed as much as those to whom we give the Light. When you practice the Divine Light Invocation always express your thanks at the end, on behalf of yourself and those who have received the Light. If you are not grateful for what you have been given it will be taken from you.

Cultivate the feeling that you are one with the Light. Be one with the Light.

Ye are the light of the World...
Let your light so shine before men,
that they may see your good works,
and glorify your Father which is in heaven.

Matthew 5:14-16

Conclusion

In conclusion, I would like to share with you some experiences of mine with the Divine Light Invocation and bring together some of the main themes of this book, especially the use of the Light Invocation as a tool for expanding awareness.

Before I decided to teach the Light Invocation to people, I weighed it very carefully back and forth in my mind. I had questioned myself many times, despite the overwhelming power of the experience in India: why had I been chosen to pass on this practice? There was no rational explanation.

One day, after I had been thinking about all of this for some time, I experienced my whole body as a mass of Light during the Light Invocation. I didn't have any specific shape or form. My body was just an outline, no more definite than the smoke of a cigarette—very faint. I had a feeling of movement; I saw my hand moving, but had no concept that I was moving my hand. It was after this that I decided that I would teach the Light Invocation to anyone who sincerely wanted to learn. I felt that if there were any misunderstanding on my part that there would be a sign, something that would prevent me from continuing to teach the Invocation.

After I had been practicing the Invocation for some years I heard a voice during my meditation: "You always determine who should have the Light, but there are many other people who also have need of it." Then I started to put people into the Light—just the figures of men, women, and children—who were in great need at that particular moment. And that has resulted in a very peculiar happening. Sometimes I can't stop the Light Invocation. The spiral of Light becomes continuous, and it's as if masses of people come running into this Light and are taken up.

Later that same week, I was sitting down meditating on the Light when suddenly I had the feeling that someone was in the room. I opened my eyes and saw a little boy about three years old, with a very warm, friendly face, standing there. When I said to him, "What can I do for you?" he just moved his shoulders, and I saw that his hands were attached to his shoulders. And I said, "Of course. I have never thought of putting all these children who are now crippled for the rest of their lives into the Light." That became part of the Light Invocation for me, and I urge other people to put those who are crippled, physically or mentally, into the Light.

Then one day I had an experience in which a voice said to me, "I want you to come with me into the dark lands." I said, "I can't see," and the voice replied, "Turn your hands toward the ground and there will be enough light from each of the hand chakras to show you where to walk." I saw that I was walking ankle-deep in mud, and that as far as my eyes could see there were babies—hundreds of thousands of babies—lying on their sides, lying on their backs, or lying face-down in the mud. All of these babies looked as if they were dead: they were not moving. And I said, "What can anybody do?" The voice answered, "They need to be loved. They need to be cared for. Put them all into the Light."

The babies were symbolic of people who need to be reborn. The experience was telling me that there are souls who need to come back to see the purpose of life and to dedicate their lives to that purpose; otherwise it is possible that they will end up becoming just pure energy. And so I also began putting into the Light those souls who need to be reborn.

For some time following these experiences, I continued to put strangers into the Light. Then I began to ask myself, "How do I know I didn't construct all of this just to make myself feel better, to feel less helpless?" I decided that if I was given some evidence, I would continue. Without some evidence I couldn't be sure that these experiences were not the result of the creativity of my mind.

It happened not long after this that I went to Oregon to visit a friend. I had only been in the house about half an hour when a telephone call came. The woman on the telephone said to my friend, "Can you give me the address of the lady swami who was here three, four, five years ago? I would like to contact her." My friend didn't say anything but just handed me the telephone!

The woman arranged to have a meeting that evening in her home and invited about thirty people. At the end of the evening the lady of the house said to me, "What is your fee, Swami Radha?" and I said, "Whatever anyone would like to give would be fine. My ticket home has already been paid." However, the woman put a large glass bowl, embarassingly large, right on top of the grand piano. People put bills into the bowl which she then placed in my lap. I didn't know how to handle this. I finally just opened my purse and began to stuff all the money in, when suddenly I saw that there was a dia-mond ring in the bowl —a very beautiful one. People were leaving so I called out, "Please wait! Someone has lost a diamond ring!" A woman's voice from the darkened entrance said, "No, Swami, the ring is for you."

I thought to myself, "What shall I do now?" People do not necessarily do these things because of inspiration. Some-times it is just emotions—perhaps they feel guilty about something, or they may be cross with their husband.

I left the ring on the mantelpiece and asked the lady of the house to telephone the owner of the ring. I thought that after she got over whatever emotions had influenced her, she would perhaps want to change her mind.

But before I could leave Oregon, I received a call. A woman's voice said, "Swami Radha, the ring was for you because of the experience I had with you." And this is what she told me. She had made a bargain. She had been having prob-lems in her family and with her husband and didn't know what to do; so she had talked to a friend who had suggested she pray about it. But the woman had said, "No, my prayers never get answered. I have given up on that."

When things went from bad to worse, her friend said, "Try praying just once more, and really put your heart into it." She decided to try once more, and that night she had an experience. She woke up around two o'clock because her room was lit up. A woman in an orange robe came in, sat on her bed, looked at her with a smile, and said, "Don't worry. Everything will be all right." She wanted to touch the woman in orange, but at that moment the figure disappeared. The Light slowly dimmed, and she went back to sleep. For weeks afterward she was in an elevated mood.

But then, she said, her mind began to doubt the experience, and she wondered if it had only been a dream. When she told her friend about her doubts, and that she wasn't quite sure what to make of the experience, the friend said, "Oh, this is very bad. You shouldn't do this. Pray again and ask the Divine to grant you just one confirmation—never ask for another one again—that you will meet this woman in orange."

The woman was in tears on the telephone and could barely talk as she said, "Last night when you came, you were that confirmation. I had promised, as my friend had also suggested, to give something precious in return for confirmation. I hadn't known why I had worn my mother's ring that evening. But when I met you, I felt I should give it to you. Please keep it."

She would not give me her name, but twelve years later I did finally meet her when she came one day to visit me at the Ashram.

And so I had my evidence that putting strangers into the Light does have an effect. We each had our evidence. But be very serious before you go into a bargain with the Divine. Be sure you are willing to keep your end of the bargain.

As you practice the Light Invocation, you will begin to express your latent powers of mind and imagination. Your emotions will become refined in a process that enables you to expand your consciousness into a state of attunement with cosmic energy, expressed here as Divine Light. Your successful participation in this process will depend greatly on how much effort you put into it. Bring all your faculties into play as you do it. Your creative participation in the Divine Light Invocation will act as an efficient therapy in three main ways:

Physically: It will have a positive effect on your health because the Light is a healing and regenerating force. By thinking of the Light and by identifying with the Light you stimulate the sustaining and energizing forces within the body. By changing your habitual physical and mental posture, even for a short time, your internal processes are beneficially reactivated.

Mentally: By inviting the activity and influence of the Divine Light, you can restore mental balance and establish a sense of proportion and perspective in your affairs. Working and identifying with the Light helps to dissolve negative thought patterns by emphasizing the positive image of Light.

Spiritually: The mind is trained to understand and perceive the reality and all-pervasiveness of higher forces, of cosmic energy in the form of Divine Light. In the light of this new understanding and growth, identification with the Light is seen to be a basic truth common to all religions.

By doing the Light Invocation you are made eligible for grace, since you express the desire to be in the Light of God. When you put another person into the Light it is important not to attach hopes, desires, or prayers. Simply see the person standing whole and healthy before you.

The Divine Light Invocation will help bring you into balance and help break the hypnotic condition of identification with the body. Many people choose to indulge in physical gratifications, to remain identified with their bodies and that level of consciousness. Realize that you are not the body, not the mind. With persistent practice the Light Invocation will help loosen mental rigidity and overcome identification with the mind. The Light is always available to you, and you can make yourself available to it. The choice is up to you.

If the light of a thousand suns
suddenly arose in the sky,
that splendor might be compared
to the radiance of the
Supreme Spirit.

Bagavadgita 11:12

Questions and Answers on The Divine Light Invocation

Q: Is it important to do the Divine Light Invocation exactly as it has been given?

Swami Radha: All spiritual practices have to be done accurately if you want to have the results. When you drive a car you can't say, "I want to take this gear differently." Third gear will not do what first does, and reverse won't go forward. In the same way, if you want a house to stand up and not have the roof fall in, then you have to build straight walls. It's all quite natural.

People have sometimes said to me, "I don't seem to get anywhere with the Light Invocation." When I ask them to show me how they do it, I have to say, "Of course. You do it your own way. You get only your own results." That means you don't get the results that the true exercise would give you. You can't say, "I would rather sit down," or, "It's uncomfortable to hold my breath." Don't make any such excuses because you will not get the power of the Light. It will not do anything. That has nothing to do with being orthodox. It means following instructions. It is one place where there is no choice. If you want it, you must surrender.

Q: Whom should I put into the Light when I do the Divine Light Invocation?

Swami Radha: Put yourself into the Light, put your family into the Light, put your children into the Light. That's where you should start when you do the Light Invocation. Whoever has been important in your life—your parents, your teachers, those who took care of you when you were young— put them all into the Light. Try to understand that those who were in charge of you did their best. And ask for the Light of understanding so that you will do better with your own children.

Anyone you love and for whom you want the very best— put that person into the Light, too. Then, with a prayerful attitude, say, "It is my desire that you grow into Light with every day." That is a spiritual gift of great value—a magnificient gift. There is nothing greater that you could give.

If you want to put a person into the Light who has already left this earth plane, you can do so as you would with anyone else. The soul on the other side will be favorably influenced and guided by the Light.

Put political leaders and governments into the Light. Fifty people putting the whole government into the Light every day, three times a day, for long enough—who knows what the effect might be?

Whenever you look at anyone or talk with anyone, practice seeing him or her in the Light. At some time later in your life your concentration will develop and you will be able to switch your thoughts to the Light at almost any time.

Remember that you are never totally helpless when it comes to other people. You can always put them into the Light.

Q: A friend of mine is having problems and I would like to help by putting her into the Light. But she is so touchy and full of resentment . . . .

Swami Radha: Touchy people shouldn't get more Light. The Light is neutral energy: touchy people may use it simply to increase their hurt and anger. But if you can first have a conversation with your friend and help her to see her touchiness, to see how she creates her own pain, to see how her criticalness breaks up her relationships, or whatever is the problem . . . . If you can lay such a foundation of understanding so that she is willing to make an effort to change, then you can support her by putting her into the Light. Then that Light will increase the effectiveness of her efforts.

If you are putting a certain person into the Light on a regular basis, keep in touch with that person, at least by letter, so that you know if your efforts are having a positive effect or not.

Q: If I channel the Light in a positive, clear way, doesn't that guarantee that the person receiving it will use it for the positive?

Swami Radha: No. I can care about someone and that person can still take advantage of me. It's the same thing. If I am putting someone into the Light in a workshop but see that the individual is using the energy for resistance, I'll stop. The energy is neutral.

Q: Then the energy is to be thought of as being neutral *and* as being positive. How can it be both?

Swami Radha: The answer to your question lies in the fourth dimension. It is as if a child were to look at the horizon and were to ask you if she could go there. How would you explain that it is not a place to which one can go? Once you have had some of your own experiences, then we will be able to talk more about these things.

Q: I have been using the image of Divine Mother as the focus for my spiritual practice; but I'm wondering if I am wrong to do so since the Divine is actually formless.

Swami Radha: You can say, "I shouldn't have any images." But being able to do without a concrete image—of Divine Mother, of the Buddha, of Jesus, of Shiva—is only possible when you have reached a high state of development. If you have an image, put that image into the Light. One day, when your mind is sufficiently trained and has learned to concentrate, you won't need these images. They will dissolve into Light because your mind will have learned to focus on something as subtle as Light. You won't have to struggle to achieve that; no particular effort will be necessary. The Light is such a subtle image that it will not interfere in your mind and keep you away from the true Cosmic Power. It will rather slowly wean you from needing an image—which is basically only helping you to focus the monkey mind.

The Divine Power has no form, no shape, no name, but we need to have some image with which to communicate, so we give it a form, shape, and name. You need to put your image of, say, Jesus into the Light so that you may realize, not the man, but what Christ Consciousness is. It's not that Jesus, God, or Divine Mother need the Light. *You* need it, so that you can dissolve that concrete image.

You won't get stuck in the worship of an image unless you want to—unless you insist that this image is a Supreme Being. If this is the case, then the idea of the Supreme Being is, at this stage in your life, essential, and so let it be until the Light dissolves it.

Sometimes the mind can become very critical and say, "I've created all this in my own mind, and there is really nothing in it." Then stop for a moment and think about how the mind *constantly* creates. At least your mind has evolved, from creating only schemes for self-gratification, to the desire to create an image of a Higher Power. Let that happen.

Q: How can I work with the Mantra of the Divine Light Invocation?

Swami Radha: Reflect upon each line of the Mantra, each word of the Mantra. What do they mean to *you*? When I say, "I am created by Divine Light," who is that I that is created by Divine Light? In the Christian teachings, God created everything. Is God Light? Is Light God? If you are "created" by Divine Light, then what is your own essential nature?

"I am sustained by Divine Light." What *does* sustain me? My emotions rob me of peace, of physical strength—so it's not my emotions that sustain me. What is my intellect doing? If I am in danger in the traffic with a car coming into my lane, it is not my intellect that solves the problem; something else takes over. In the Christian teachings it says, "Man does not live by bread alone."* That divine spark that each one of us has, that is what sustains me.

If you are "protected" by Divine Light and "surrounded" by Divine Light, what is there to fear? Have yourself surrounded by Divine Light wherever you are, wherever you go. Surround others with the Divine Light. Let the Light also shine through your eyes.

"I am ever growing into Divine Light." In the last sentence of the affirmation you state that you have chosen to grow into the Light, that you wish to evolve and to cooperate with the divine law in the course of your own spiritual evolution, which is your purpose in living.

The Mantra of the Light actually has only four lines. But one time I spontaneously said, "If I could constantly be growing into Light, then things would be all right. Then nothing would be able to stop me"; so I added the fifth line, "I am ever growing into Divine Light," and it has become part of

*Matthew, 4:4

the Mantra. However, I always feel obliged to let everyone know that the original Mantra ended at four lines.

You can find your own fifth line—to express what it is that you want for yourself—or you can use mine; but then put all your will behind it.

It is not so easy to let go of all the desires that we have, but we can take one desire and let that hover over all the others: "I am ever growing into Light."

If the Mantra is just some words that you say mechanically, that's not good enough. You have to clarify the meaning for yourself as best you can, and on more than an intellectual level—on a level that goes beyond the words. Feelings and emotions must also be involved. It must not be an empty repetition, even though in the course of many years this also would bear fruit. It's like a tree: if you don't water it, the fruit may be small, undeveloped, and dry. But when you take care of a tree and give it water, the fruit comes out in its season, ripe and juicy. Whatever you put into an endeavor, that is what you will get out of it.

Q: I am not able to visualize the Light at all when I do the Divine Light Invocation, but I can feel it. Is that good enough?

Swami Radha: You are probably more of a feeling person. It's useful to know which one of your senses dominates. People who have a keen sense of hearing may neither see nor feel the Light; they may simply hear it, as a hissing sound.

You should always try to involve intense feelings when doing the Light Invocation, so that with practice you can feel the Light entering into your physical body. But it's important to balance all your senses, and to bring the other senses into the picture. It's not helpful to be always only in your feelings. You have to have inner vision in order to have a vision of your future; so you have to practice visualization.

You can hang up a naked light bulb and stand under it. Or when you take a shower, visualize the shower as the Light. Use some of the visualization exercises that I have given in this book, or invent your own. You will be able to visualize eventually if you keep practicing the Light Invocation.

Q: I know that some people feel the Light as a warmth in the palms of their hands. But I feel it in my heart center. Is that all right?

Swami Radha: Yes, fine! That's good! This is where things differ from individual to individual.

Q: What does it mean that I feel the energy coming from the area of the solar plexus when I do the Light Invocation?

Swami Radha: You are giving, then, from your emotions. I'm very careful to envision my whole physical body as Light. I try to see myself as skin, with nothing inside—just my outer skin, like a balloon that I fill with Light. Then I can usually keep most of my emotions out.

Q: When I visualize someone standing in the Light

during the Light Invocation, should I try to imagine the person exactly as he or she really looks?

Swami Radha: Only briefly. You want to focus on the Light. See the person as if he or she were a glass figure filled with liquid Light.

I will tell you about an experience I had. One day I was sitting in meditation doing the Light Invocation in my mind as I would do it physically, imagining myself standing up and tensing the muscles and so on. Suddenly in that meditation I saw a kind of oversized human figure. It was like a figure from an anatomy book: it had no particular features, but I could see its nerves and blood vessels. It was very fine—almost like a Japanese drawing; it was almost disappearing in Light. I realized that this is how I must see people in the Light Invocation.

Q: Sometimes when I do the Light Invocation and imagine someone in the Light, the person doesn't seem to go up. Is that because of something I am doing wrong, or is that saying something about the person?

Swami Radha: You can only find this out with reasonable certainty if you observe yourself and keep a regular diary. That was my only way of finding out. You have to know your own reactions and your own attachments very well. You cannot know if your criticism is holding a person down unless you have sufficient awareness of where you are critical. But if it happens with a total stranger, someone you haven't even met and with whom you have no particular emotional involvement except your desire to help, then you can be sure that the problem is that the person is "heavy." Such a person needs to do more work on himself.

If I arrive at the conclusion that the problem could very well be my critical attitude toward the person, I simply acknowledge that this is the way I feel right now. Acknowledging one's criticalness can make a difference, can even totally resolve the difficulty. Sometimes, through the repeated actions of the individual, my resentment comes back. Sometimes more Light has to come to me first, to dissolve my resentment, my criticism. I have feelings like everyone else, but I do not let them rule me. I never say, "You're not worth putting into the Light—I'm not going to waste my time on you."

All of our minds work differently. When I have this problem, there seems to be a black shadow preventing me from seeing the person clearly. Know your own mind and how it operates.

It also can take place that a person goes up into the Light too quickly and too straight. This can mean that the individual is passing from this earth plane into another life—that means death.

Q: I feel weakened after doing the Light Invocation.

Swami Radha: I cannot stress enough that the effects of the practice can also be negative. That can happen when you allow the ego to take over and you think that you give the Light *from your self*. In so doing, you may lose your own reserves and become weakened instead of becoming physically, mentally, and emotionally invigorated. Therefore, you must at all times remember that the energy is not going out from you, but flowing through you.

Q: What if my concentration on a certain day is poor in spite of my best efforts? Should I still do the Light Invocation?

Swami Radha: You can still do the Invocation, but say to the Divine, "My concentration was poor, but that's all that I can give today. You have to do the rest."

And you will see that you can go away with a light heart, because you have not tried to pretend in any way. That is important.

Q: Can the Light Invocation help me when I am feeling an emotion such as anger or hatred?

Swami Radha: When you have an emotion such as hatred, immediately put yourself and whomever you feel that way toward into the Light. If your hate or dislike is from the past, because of someone disappointing you, hurting you, or letting you down, put that person into the Light. Rather than being angry, feel sorry for that person. How can I scold you for not giving me a million dollars when you haven't even one dollar? In other words, if you haven't even one dollar's worth of goodness in you, how can I ask you for a million dollar's worth, or for fifty, or for two? I have to be intelligent enough to recognize that I cannot demand of you what you haven't got. Hate won't change that. Anger won't change that. Frustration won't change that. Jealousy won't change that.

If I fight my anger or if I fight my jealousy, I get involved with anger, I get involved with jealousy. When you realize something isn't right in yourself, don't get into a fight with it, because then you get involved with the negative. Make a decision to remove the negative, and as soon as you have made the decision, invite the Light in. "That is gone. Now the door is open." Be open, fully open, to the Light.

Give the negative recognition—don't sweep it under the carpet. Recognize, "Yes, I am angry. Yes, I am jealous. Yes, I am greedy." But then shift your focus to something that will nourish you, that will help you. Shift your focus to the Light. Let all these negative aspects dissolve in the Light.

The first week I was in India, my Guru, Swami Sivananda, brought me a cup of black coffee. He started pouring milk into the coffee and as he poured, the coffee got lighter and lighter until finally you really couldn't have known that the cup had originally held black coffee.

Swami Sivananda didn't pour all the black coffee out. You can't jump over your own shadow: you have to accept yourself the way you are. But pour the milk in. Pour the Divine Light in. And finally the transformation is going to take place.

Q: I am finding that difficult, unresolved issues from my past are suddenly beginning to come up. I have been doing the Light Invocation regularly for some time: could there be a connection?

Swami Radha: In the course of time, as you practice the Divine Light Invocation, sudden insights into many things will come to you—perhaps things of a long-forgotten past. If these are things that you have been trying to forget, you will now be able to look at them, deal with them, and put them aside. The Divine Light will dissolve negative, unconscious influences from the past and you will not have to dwell on them.

If you think more deeply about it, even a small flash of light makes us aware of the darkness around us, of the darkness within us—in our minds or in our hearts. It is like taking a match into a basement or a medieval cellar that no one has cleaned for decades: in the flash of that match, what has accumulated in the darkness becomes visible. It is only when we make a conscious effort to know what is in the depths of the unconscious, where everything is stuffed away in a disorderly manner, that we really can see how much work it will take to do that cleaning-up job. In the beginning, each Light Invocation is like a match showing us for a few brief moments what needs to be done. Let this create the desire in you to be only in the Light, to move closer to the Light.

On a daily, practical level, to live in the Light means to have nothing to hide. Then you don't need to be nervous about being found out, and that is essential if you are to have true inner peace. But if you do have something to hide, put it in the Light. The Light will take care of it. Wrong actions have their source in the darkness; therefore it is extremely important to be in the Light.

Q: Is it necessary that I be in perfect health myself in order to be a healing channel of the Light for others?

Swami Radha: No, the state of health of the channel is not important. The attitude, the inspiration, the hope, and the compassion will overrule any weak or afflicted part of your own body.

Q: Why do some people become healed, or at least improve, and others do not, even when repeated efforts have been made?

Swami Radha: Two of the most common reasons are these: the person who is to be healed may have been conditioned to believe that such healing is not possible; or the individual may be suffering from low self-esteem, feeling unworthy of being healed and illumined by Divine Light.

We also should not expect spiritual healing if the person makes no effort to find out if he or she is violating the laws of nature. Sometimes we make ourselves sick through wrong action, or even wrong food. You owe it to yourself to investigate what is good for your body and what isn't. Take responsibility for your actions, for what you do, for what you eat. And encourage anyone you think you should put in the Light to do the same. We cannot expect the Divine to take care of our own laziness. Ask for the Light of understanding to remove the obstacle. What the Light Invocation may do is bring the individual in contact with people who will help the person recognize where the error lies.

Pain is a great teacher. For many people, pain is the only teacher they will listen to. The sick person may need to be sick in order to learn something. And how few people pray when they are happy, when they are healthy. How few think to contact their best friend when everything is in perfect order. Most of the time we turn to the Divine when we are in despair, when we suffer, when there is pain.

Any help offered, either through the Divine Light Invocation or through other methods such as the laying on of hands, should not be given without discrimination. Humility, devotion, and gratitude are major ingredients for well-being. The desire to give back to life—to give selfless service—is also necessary. If these ingredients are lacking, the person serving as a channel has to awaken in the individual an understanding of the need for these finer emotions. If there is no proper sense of gratitude in the healed person—that is, one that is spontaneous and from the heart—it can be expected that the illness will come back or another will manifest.

The person must also have the desire to be healed and to accept the ups and downs, the challenges, of life.

In the case of a serious illness some pertinent questions should be asked, such as, What is the purpose of your life? What kind of person do you want to be? What do you want to give back to life?

The person may first have to grow in the Light of understanding before the Light of healing will come. If I put you into the Light you may suddenly, or in time, realize what you are doing. The Light of love may also have to come before the Light of healing, if you are so egocentric that you love only yourself.

Many diseases and emotional pain come about through the power of suggestion, which is the result of uncultivated thinking and of habits. The power of suggestion should be thoroughly understood by a helper. If the person to be healed has used self-suggestion in a destructive way, it is very important to bring about this understanding before replacing the old suggestions with new, constructive ones.

Q: Can I be a channel of healing for others if I am still full of anger and other negative emotions myself?

Swami Radha: You have to absorb the Light first before you can become a channel for the divine force. That means you have to first remove the "debris" in yourself. If you have a water pipe, and if there is a lot of debris in the water, you have to have a strainer in the pipe to catch it. And if it is plugged up, you have to take it out and rinse it and clear it. Otherwise you put all your own emotions, your own resentments, your own bitterness or pain, into the other person. Unless these emotions are removed, the healing will just not take place.

Q: Isn't it helpful to touch the person in need of healing?

Swami Radha: Most people don't know how to be a channel. Through touch, they put their own emotional garbage and their own problems into the already weakened and very sensitive and receptive body. You don't need to touch anybody. Put them into the Light.

Q: Can I teach the Divine Light Invocation to others?

Swami Radha: Yes, but first make sure that you can do it accurately yourself. When you show others how to do the practice, do it with them, and be sure they know how to first fill their whole body, and all levels of their being, with Light.

Then let them share this Light with anyone they would like to help or bless. Make sure that they can repeat the Invocation properly. When you teach people the Light Invocation you can have that assured feeling, particularly after you have done it for a while yourself, that you have given a valid tool from the best of your knowledge.

Q: I am often in a counselling and teaching role. How can I use the Divine Light Invocation?

Swami Radha: I demand of all people who want to counsel others and to get some background at the Ashram, that they do a certain amount of spiritual practice, so that they transcend the level of general psychology. I find out if they can keep a conversation going with their client and at the same time see the person in the Light, so that they remain a channel. If they can't, I tell them to have a clipboard on which they draw a little sun and to keep this in front of them when they're with their clients until they reach the point where they remember the Light—where all conversation, all involvement with the person who has the problems, will not cut them off from the memory of and the contact with the Light. That is important. And when you take a client to the door, you can say, "Never forget you were created by Divine Light and you are sustained by Divine Light."

In helping people, we often don't know if we did the right thing. After any interview or workshop that you give, put everybody into the Light and put yourself into the Light.

Q: I teach Hatha Yoga. I would like to introduce the

Light Invocation to my classes, but I don't think they are ready to accept it.

Swami Radha: You can teach people to do the breathing, coordinated with tensing and relaxing the body, without saying anything about the Light. This alone will be a wonderful help to them. It is not only quite rejuvenating, but it will help them think into their bodies.

There is also no question that we have more concentration when we tense our muscles and hold our breath. Wherever you are, if you need to become single-pointed, you can tense your body and hold your breath. Babaji's teaching me this practice was a real God-given blessing. It is only through this particular method that I was able to get my own mind under control whenever I needed to do so.

Q: Can the Divine Light Invocation help me with my fear of death?

Swami Radha: Your attachment to the body: this creates a fear of dying. Realize that there *is* no death. You just go from *this* room . . . to *that* room! This room is the world; it has limitations. When death comes, you just move into another room. Break the limitations. Live a life without fear.

Death is there at any moment, not just when we get older. It's not just someone who has cancer who is a terminal case. We are all "terminal cases," every one of us. But if you understand the world of Divine Light, then you go into something that has a greater reality.

Do not allow your intellect to be the cancer that eats away at your knowledge of the Light. Do not let the intellect nibble away at what you know inside by intuition. Your intuition is more correct than your intellect. Your intellect reflects physical fear, but your intuition has the glimpse of the Light. It is the mind that will not allow a true reflection of the Light. Therefore breath has to be calmed. When there is no wind, no air, no breath on the lake, the reflection is beautiful. The mind is like a lake. When you still the waves of the mind, then you reflect your original Self, that which you really are.

Death is not losing consciousness. It's rather gaining consciousness, and becoming aware of the Light, if the preparation for the physical death has been done correctly. If we are so much absorbed in Light that little else has importance for us, then at the time of death we pass into the Light. If we are absorbed in Light, facing death is not really all that difficult. We simply take off the clothes that no longer fit us.

I shall have no regrets about dying, because I know that the daily consciousness that we have, the body consciousness or *bodymind* is keeping us from the Light. It's the bodymind that creates all these clouds, all these illusions that hide the Light or that make us forget the Light.

The mind is a phenomenon indeed, and so is the body. This whole world is a big phenomenon. What you consider real today, in a little while you will realize was your own illusion, your own expectations, your own desires to have it be that way. Once your illusions have burst like soap bubbles, not much is left to bind you. Then why not go home?

Can you see the Light in your food? In another person? Can the Divine in you salute the Divine in the other? It is even possible to salute the Divine in each other in the most intimate and secret moments. Can you bring that Light into every aspect of your life? Then you will not be so concerned with what happens to your body. Let the body dissolve into Light. When it is time for my body to dissolve into Light, I will gladly let that Light take over. Let the Light come into your life, into every cell of your body, into every level of your emotions, into every level of your feelings, into every level of your thinking, into every level of your intellect. You cannot be anything else, someday. Then be a ray of that Light *now*.

Q: I had an experience of the Light. But now that it has faded, I wonder if it was just something my mind created.

Swami Radha: When you think you have had a spiritual experience, but it is only your mind that has created it, then you can recreate it. When it comes from a different source, you cannot recreate it. And a true spiritual experience will leave you changed.

When the experience fades, you can cherish the memory. The memory is like the back of a piece of embroidery: you can see the pattern, but in a somewhat different or less clear way.

If any one of you does the Light Invocation with 100 percent concentration, no additional thoughts of self-importance coming in by the back door, at that moment—and I grant you this—you will experience your body as a mass of Light. Let this be the sugar candy that tempts you; you cannot resist sugar candy that is Light! That other sugar is gone so fast—why would you even go after it? It is not worth your energy, not worth the time and the effort.

But remember that there is no experience that will stay with you forever. Experiences come and go. You may even forget all about the experience; but then a nagging feeling will come that says, "You have forgotten, you have drifted away. Hurry back to your heavenly home."

The experience of one's body being a mass of Light is not the end, but it is a confirmation that you are doing the right thing.

Q: Can the Light Invocation affect me when I am asleep?

Swami Radha: You should be in the Light not only in your waking state, but even in your sleep. Before you get into bed, you should do the complete Divine Light Invocation and spin a cocoon of Light around your bed. Then you can slide into that cocoon of Light as you slide under the covers. Knowing that your body is now protected by the Light, you can ask that your Higher Self be of help during the night to anyone in need.

If you focus on the Light as you are falling asleep, you will very likely stay with the Light for most of the night. This means that you must watch yourself falling asleep, so that you can put yourself in the Light at the very last moment. This is not easy because before you realize it, you are already asleep.

If you have nightmares, you can use your vivid imagination to your benefit by putting yourself into the Light. You will see that your fear will go. Much fear is uncultivated imagination.

One day in meditation I saw a human figure filled with liquid Light. Then only the head appeared to me, and I saw that the brain was a luminous mass. That luminosity represented, for me, the Divine Light, which is probably with us when we are born. Then I saw that colorful little lights were shooting at the brain from all directions. Wherever they touched the brain, the Light went out, until it was sprinkled with dark spots. This image repeated itself a few times and was so powerful that it never left me.

When I began to observe these colorful little lights, I became aware that although they were exciting, they did not have an aura of the Light; they had rather an aura of the death of the Light. I began to wonder if, by the time most people go to bed, the luminosity of the brain is gone. Whatever you do, half an hour before you go to sleep, you should do something that nourishes that luminosity or that brings it back. This includes the kind of thoughts you entertain. Even if you have a serious reason to be critical of someone's actions, you should counterbalance that critical thought. If you don't counterbalance it, it will destroy some of the luminosity of the brain until eventually there will be nothing left. And that is a very bad situation for anyone to be in.

Q: Sometimes I ask the Divine for an answer to a problem, but nothing seems to come.

Swami Radha: When emotions are running high and your personality aspects are at war within yourself, there is no way you will receive an answer. First you must still your mind. I suggest you first chant a Mantra,* to express the emotions through your voice and your breath. Then, when your breath has calmed down, do some 4-16-8 pranayama.** Once you have become even quieter, do the Light Invocation in order to establish the proper identification, even if you just go through the Invocation in your mind while you are sitting. Finally, do the meditation on the pinpoint of Light.***

The Divine Light Invocation—visualizing yourself filled with Light—is the most effective, powerful, and potent exercise you can do; because your problem is that you suffer from the wrong identification. You say to yourself, "I'm not good enough. I need So-and-so's approval." Identify only with the Divine. Seek only the approval of the Divine.

I have also at times asked one of the Gurus whom I have known to be the channel for an answer. You can do that. But eventually you have to learn to quiet your mind and your emotions so that you can hear that still, small voice within yourself. Then that will give you the right answer.

Q: I have trouble doing the Light Invocation because I don't really feel worthy of being a channel for the Light.

Swami Radha: A diamond is a diamond, even when it is in the rough. To help break your poor self-image, think of

*See *Mantras: Words of Power*, by Swami Sivananda Radha, 1980, Timeless Books, for complete instructions on the use of Mantra.
**See *Kundalini: Yoga for the West*, by Swami Sivananda Radha,1978, Timeless Books, pages 211-217, for an explanation of this type of pranayama.
***See *Guided Meditation*, a cassette tape by Swami Sivananda Radha, available from Timeless Books.

yourself as a diamond in the process of being polished—or as a Cadillac, stuck in the mud, covered in mud. Take a hose and wash the mud off it. Discover the beauty that is underneath. Look for that ember of Light inside you. Keep that alive and try to encourage that little Light, so that it will become a good, strong flame.

If you create a spiritual bank account and put into it all of your Light Invocations, you are bound to get interest. So when are you going to open your account? Once you have a spiritual bank account, you know what you have; you don't have to prove anything to anyone.

Remember that I was not an angel when I went to India and was given the Divine Light Invocation. This should be obvious from my India diary which describes that period in my life.* If *I* could experience the Light, with all my shortcomings, so can you.

Q: I want to experience the Light, but I have so many other desires in my life . . . .

Swami Radha: To be entirely desireless is impossible. You desire to eat, to breathe, to keep the body alive. Even wanting to attain to a higher state is a desire.

But elevate your desires. The desire for the Most High,

---

*See *Radha:Diary of a Woman's Search*, by Swami Sivananda Radha, 1981, Timeless Books.

the desire for the Inner Light, that longing—that is what you have to cultivate. That is where you have to focus.

If you want name and fame, then there is nothing more for you to attain to, because you will be satisfied with that. But if you desire Divine Light, then *that* will be your reward.

If it is another person that you want, remember that any person will let you down at one time or another. Each person has to go his or her own way; another's development isn't necessarily running parallel to yours. People part ways, but the Divine will never part.

You cannot want the Most High just because you are dissatisfied with what you have—with your husband, your wife, your job. This can propel you into asking if there isn't more to life; but you must want the Light for its own sake. It is like love: you must love for love's sake and not because you want to be loved back. This would be altogether the wrong attitude.

Make contact with that Inner Light and desire that Inner Light only.

Q: I have been doing the Light Invocation for five years, but now I realize that I have been doing it mechanically. I think it would be easier for me if I could think of the Light as divine love.

Swami Radha: Never let your spiritual practice fall into mechanicalness or you won't experience any benefits. Five years gone by . . . and nothing. That is sad. It is also a serious injury that you bring on yourself when you do that. We may fail many times, but as long as we keep up our interaction with the Divine, then we will have "eternal life." But if we let that die out, that is sin. We may not be given that opportunity again.

If you had done the Light Invocation with real attention, giving the best of yourself to it, you would have experienced the Light of understanding; and from the Light of understanding, the Light of love is bound to come.

Q: Can a group of people do the Light Invocation?

Swami Radha: Sometimes you may wish to increase the power of the Light by inviting your friends and relatives to invoke the Light with you. In this particular situation, one of you should speak the Mantra aloud as an affirmation; everyone else should repeat it mentally. If the individual who is to be put into the Light is one of this group, let him or her step forward into the center of the circle.

If you cannot actually get together with others to do the practice, you can arrange to do the Invocation at the same time that day. This is also very helpful.

Q: The Divine Light Invocation is such a brief practice. Isn't chanting a Mantra or meditating for a few hours more effective?

Swami Radha: What is important is how much you involve yourself in what you do, how much you are *with* the practice. Some people have to meditate four, five, six hours a day. But that is not everyone's way. Let us say you chant for four hours a day for four years. Unless you really give yourself to it, it's not any different from washing dishes three times a day for four years. If prolonged periods of spiritual practice alone would do it, all the people who have spent years and years in monasteries would be saints. What counts is how much of yourself you put into it—because that is what you will get out of it. When you do the Light Invocation, really be there with every fiber of your being. That is what will get you there.

Q: Can doing the Light Invocation, for myself or for others, interfere with karma,* that is, prevent a person from learning his or her lessons?

Swami Radha: Yes, it can. But only if you get your will, your own desires, in the way. I personally would not interfere, because each person should find out what his or her karma is. If I were shortsighted I would not immediately say, "I want my eyes healed." First I want to know where I am "short-sighted" and what it is that I don't want to see; otherwise the karma will still be there—not as a punishment, but because the real problem has not been corrected. My experience in doing the Light Invocation has been that I get the Light of understanding about the karmic problem, and then I act on that.

I do not attach any hopes or desires to the Light Invocation and say, "He *must* get well." That's why I like the Light Invocation: it gives me a chance to help without telling God what to do. The Divine Light Invocation will do for the person

---

*Karma, in this context, refers to the effects on one's life of one's past actions, and to the life-lessons one has to learn.

whatever that person needs—and still be within the will of God.

Q: Yet you recommend, when we see a sick person in the Light, that we visualize the person as "healthy." Isn't that a form of telling the Divine what to do?

Swami Radha: No, it is just that it is important not to hold a crippled image of the person in my mind, *preventing* the person from getting well.

Q: It seems to me that if God has a plan for me or for someone else, then that plan is going to unfold itself. What does the Light Invocation do?

Swami Radha: It makes you eligible for grace. Because you express the will to be in the Light of God, you open yourself to the Light of God. Doing the Light Invocation for someone else, it is as if you were pleading for that person in court.

Q: How can I keep aware of the Light during the day? I get so caught up in other things.

Swami Radha: Link any kind of light with Divine Light—when you sit in the sun, or when you watch the sun rise in the early morning, or when you light a candle.

Put little notes all over your house that say "I am not the body. I am not the mind. I am Light eternal." Add it to your bathroom mirror. I used to have it on my typewriter. I had it anywhere you could think of.

Put up pictures of suns, of light. Draw pictures of suns or embroider suns. Be creative and use your imagination to think up ways to remind yourself of the Light. It's not that we're so bad; it's that we forget. Especially in the West with all our activities, we keep forgetting.

Bring the Light into your work. Do the Light Invocation and put your work into the Light—make it an offering. This is especially helpful if you have work that is disagreeable to you. To overcome that feeling, do the Light Invocation.

Surrendering to the Light, if sustained, guarantees that eventually the Light will stay. Then, since not all the Light is needed at all times, you can turn the Light brighter or dimmer: it is as if you had a dimmer switch.

Make it a point at least once every day to do the Light Invocation with every bit of concentration that you can put into it, so that you will remember your divine nature, so that you will *experience* your divine nature.

Q: I find the Light Invocation difficult.

Swami Radha: The Light Invocation is not really as simple as it often appears to be. There are many points of concentration, and while focusing on one, you must not lose the others. In other words, every pore of your skin has to be concentrated on what you do, in order to receive that Light.

Babaji said to teach the Invocation to everyone. This means that he must give it his very special power; otherwise it would not have happened that people with very little ability to concentrate have still had results.

Often the reason we have little power to concentrate is that our emotions skim off all the power. There is nothing left to concentrate *with*.

Some of the focal points in the Invocation are:
> the tension and relaxation in the body
> the breath
> the Mantra
> the image of Light
> the feeling of Light
> the point between the eyebrows
> a general awareness as to whether the
> Light is present or has faded.

Focus first on one thing, then on another and so on, adding these points as you would pick flowers to add to the ones that you already have in your hand, until you have a bunch.

Q: Did you ever have any further experiences of Babaji?

Swami Radha: In the early years, when I first came back from India and was teaching the Light Invocation to everyone as I had been instructed to do, every now and then I would ask myself, "Why me? Why was *I* given this practice? I am not so pure or so holy. Perhaps I should not be teaching this. Perhaps it was all the fabrication of my mind." In those days I did not tell anyone the story of how Babaji had given me the Light Invocation. I kept that secret.

Then it began to happen that when I would teach the Light Invocation to a group of people—at the Self-Realization Fellowship, at the Association for Research and Enlightenment, in churches—someone would often come up to me afterward and say something like, "Have you ever read Yogananda's *Autobiography of a Yogi?*"* Then the person would tell me that he or she had seen Babaji, whose picture is in this book, standing right behind me, or beside me, as I had been teaching the practice.

This happened to me so many times that finally I had to accept that my original experience with Babaji had been genuine. I was also grateful to the Divine for giving me the reassurance, that I was doing the right thing in teaching the Light Invocation, and that I shouldn't worry that my own shortcomings were a hindrance.

But you see for you it is only a story. You may feel inspired, and you may feel impressed, but ten years from now having heard *my* story won't have made you any different. You have to get your own story. You have to keep doing the Light Invocation until you get results from it, no matter how long it takes.

* See *Autobiography of a Yogi*, by Paramhansa Yogananda, chapter 33.

Other books by
SWAMI SIVANANDA RADHA

Radha: Diary of a Woman's Search
Kundalini: Yoga for the West
Hatha Yoga: The Hidden Language
The Hatha Yoga Workbook
Mantras: Words of Power
Seeds of Light

An audio tape giving the full instructions for the Divine Light Invocation is also available from:

Timeless Books
Box 50905
Palo Alto, CA 94303-0673
(415)321-8311 or (604)227-9224

Write or call for our free catalogue of books, audio tapes, video tapes and more.